THIS IS THE ACCOUNT OF NOAH AND HIS FAMILY.

AS MANKIND GREW IN NUMBERS ON THE FACE OF THE EARTH, THEY TURNED THEIR FACE AWAY FROM GOD.

GOD SAW THIS, AND WAS GRIEVED.

BUT GOD ALSO SAW NOAH...

NOAH HAD THREE SONS: SHEM, HAM, AND JAPHETH.

QUICKLY, BROTHERS. LET'S GET WHAT WE NEED AND GET HOME.

THESE SUPPLIES FATHER ASKED US TO BUY? I'VE NEVER SEEN SUCH A LIST!

HE'S JUST TRYING TO PREPARE FOR ANY EVENTUALITY. THE WORK IS ALMOST COMPLETE!

GENESIS 6-9

GENESIS 6-9-10

GENESIS 6-13

NOAH! NOAH! GUESS WHAT? YOU'RE FINALLY GOING TO GET SOME MORE HELP ON THIS PROJECT!

I TOLD YOU, MY LOVE, WE'RE NOT GOING TO HIRE OR BUY HELP!

THAT'S NOT WHAT I MEAN!

THEN WHAT DO YOU... OH...

OH!!!

DO YOU MEAN...

CRASH

YES, NOAH!

YES!!!

"MY BROTHERS AND I WERE BORN TO THIS LIFE.

"WE LEARNED OF FATHER'S MISSION AS SOON AS WE LEARNED TO TALK.

"THERE WAS MUCH WE DID NOT UNDERSTAND.

"WE TOOK PART IN HIS VISION AS SOON AS WE LEARNED TO WALK.

"BUT THIS MUCH WE KNEW: IF GOD TOLD OUR FATHER TO BUILD THE BOAT AND TO SAVE OUR FAMILY, WE WERE GOING TO DO EVERYTHING IN OUR STRENGTH TO HELP MAKE IT HAPPEN.

GENESIS 6:18

GENESIS 6:5

AND WHEN THE ARK WAS FINISHED, GOD SPOKE TO NOAH ONCE MORE.

NEVER IMAGINED IT'D BE FINISHED!

ALL MY LIFE!

WHAT ARE WE GOING TO DO TOMORROW?

I'LL STILL DREAM ABOUT CUTTING WOOD TONIGHT, I BET!

QUIET! EVERYONE!

NOAH, WHERE'S THE WATER I SENT YOU TO GET?

WHERE'S THE WATER, YOU ASK? HA! IT'S COMING! I HEARD THE VOICE OF GOD AGAIN!

HE TOLD ME TO TAKE YOU INTO THE ARK.

WE'RE TO TAKE SEVEN OF EVERY KIND OF CLEAN ANIMAL, A MALE AND ITS MATE--

--AND TWO OF EVERY KIND OF UNCLEAN ANIMAL, A MALE AND ITS MATE--

--TO KEEP THEIR VARIOUS KINDS ALIVE THROUGHOUT THE EARTH.

"SEVEN DAYS FROM NOW, HE WILL SEND RAIN ON THE EARTH FOR FORTY DAYS AND FORTY NIGHTS!"

HOW ARE WE SUPPOSED TO ROUND UP ALL THOSE ANIMALS?

WILL OUR WORK EVER BE DONE?

SEVEN DAYS! SEVEN DAYS!?!

"AGAIN, HE TOLD ME HOW HE WILL WIPE FROM THE FACE OF THE EARTH EVERY LIVING CREATURE HE HAS MADE."

GENESIS 6:19-22

GENESIS 6:19-20

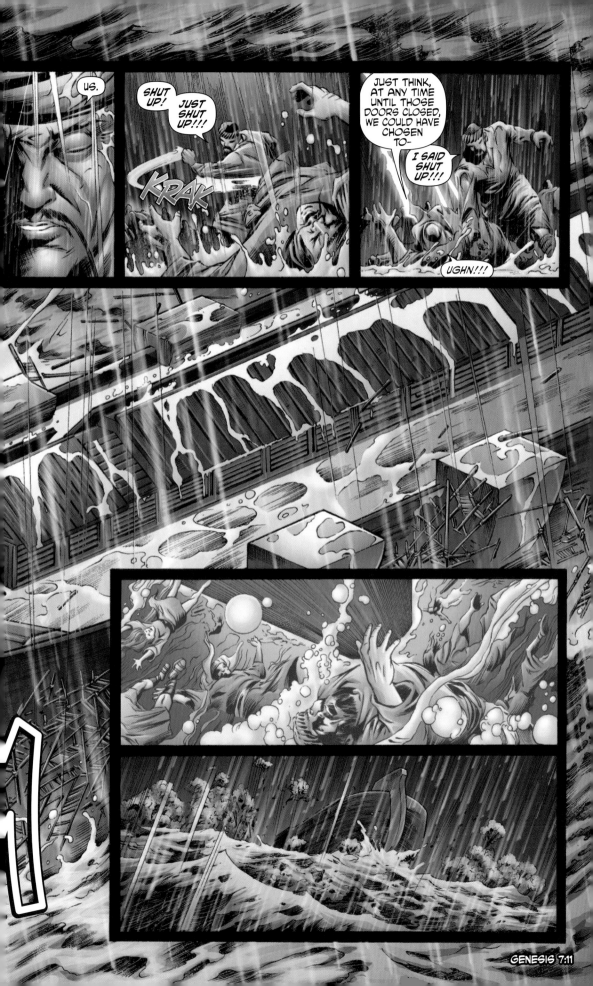

THE ARK WAS AGROUND FOR OVER ONE HUNDRED DAYS WHEN NOAH SENT A RAVEN.

WHY DID YOU DO THAT, FATHER?

FROM THE HEIGHTS, THE RAVEN SHOULD BE ABLE TO FIND DRY LAND. IF HE COMES BACK, WE'LL KNOW THAT THE WATERS HAVEN'T—

NO, FATHER, I MEANT WHY DID YOU SEND ONE OF THE RAVENS? WE ONLY HAVE TWO OF THEM, AND IF SOMETHING HAPPENS TO THAT ONE...

AH, YES. UH, GOOD POINT.

MAYBE I'LL SEND A DOVE, NEXT TIME. WE'VE GOT SEVEN OF THEM...

BUT THE RAVEN COULD ONLY FLY BACK AND FORTH OVER THE WATERS.

A WEEK LATER...

WHY BOTHER, FATHER? YOU SENT THE RAVEN LAST WEEK AND THAT DIDN'T REVEAL ANYTHING.

YES, BUT I'M CURIOUS. I WANT TO KNOW WHAT THINGS ARE LIKE OUTSIDE, BUT I DARE NOT RISK OPENING THE DOOR!

GENESIS 8:6-9

BRING OUT EVERY KIND OF LIVING CREATURE THAT IS WITH YOU—THE BIRDS, THE ANIMALS, AND ALL THE CREATURES THAT MOVE ALONG THE GROUND—SO THEY CAN MULTIPLY ON THE EARTH AND BE FRUITFUL AND INCREASE IN NUMBER UPON IT.

GENESIS 8:17-19

SONG! GATHER ONE OF EACH OF THE CLEAN ANIMALS!

WHY, FATHER?

THEY WILL BE OFFERED TO OUR GOD AS A SACRIFICE.

NOW, A FIRE.

A DOVE, FATHER.

GENESIS 9:11-17

NOAH AND HIS FAMILY SET TO WORK.

WORKING THE EARTH.

BUILDING HOUSES.

TENDING TO THE BEASTS.

MAKING THEIR NEW LIFE.

FEELS GOOD TO BUILD SOMETHING THAT WILL BE FINISHED IN A DAY OR TWO FOR A CHANGE, EH, BROTHERS?

AND NOAH PLANTED A VINEYARD.

FEELS GOOD TO BUILD SOMETHING THAT DOESN'T REQUIRE CLIMBING FORTY-FIVE FOOT TALL SCAFFOLDING!

DRINKING THE WINE, HE BECAME DRUNK.

MMM. GOOD. SWEET.

IF YOU THINK ABOUT IT, THOUGH, WE'RE BUILDING THIS TENT FOR THE SAME REASON WE BUILT THE ARK: TO STAY DRY!

GENESIS 9:20-21

FATHER?

MOTHER WONDERS IF YOU WOULD—

OH, FATHER!

I WAS HOPING THOSE BIRDS WOULD STAY AROUND HERE.

THEY LOOKED LIKE THEY HAD GOOD MEAT, BUT THEY LEFT WITH ALL THE OTHER ANIMALS.

HAM, WHAT'S WRONG?

ASK FATHER WHAT'S WRONG!

THE VINEYARD THAT HE PLANTED HAS YIELDED ITS CROP, APPARENTLY, AND OUR FATHER IS DRUNK ON IT!

NOW HE LIES IN HIS TENT, NAKED AS THE DAY HE WAS BORN!

SEE FOR YOURSELF!

GENESIS 9:23-27

AND NOAH'S FAMILY GREW. HIS SONS HAD SONS OF THEIR OWN.

FATHER! IT'S A BOY! WE'RE GOING TO NAME HIM ARAM! MY WIFE IS FINE, THE WOMEN ARE TENDING TO HER!

BUT I WANTED YOU TO SEE YOUR FIRST GRANDSON!

ARAM.

A WICKED GENERATION IS GONE, BUT THE WICKEDNESS-OUR WICKEDNESS-IS NOT.

WE HAVE A COVENANT WITH GOD THAT HE WILL NOT AGAIN CLEANSE THE EARTH WITH A FLOOD.

I WONDER, WHAT COVENANT WILL GOD MAKE WITH THE FUTURE GENERATIONS TO CLEANSE THEIR SINS?

AND FROM THESE FAMILIES, THE CLANS AND THE NATIONS OF THE WORLD SPREAD OVER THE EARTH AFTER THE FLOOD...

GENESIS 9:19, 28